# *nths client satyr—*

*prose quart-rains.*

**Peter Ganick**

**2014**
**LUNA BISONTE PRODS**

***nths client satyr—***
***prose quart-rains.***
**Peter Ganick**



ISBN 978-1-938521-16-4

Cover credits:
John M. Bennett and C. Mehrl Bennett
collaborations

LUNA BISONTE PRODS
137 Leland Ave.
Columbus OH 43214 USA

johnmbennett.net
https://www.lulu.com/lunabisonteprods

a rogue wander in zone contrarian fluster mode from accordance to prelude imperious caftan mirror 'gainst circuitry bloke rename valse oreilles dreadlocks nuage

toon official procession gavel imitate loquaciously root canopy there sudden-songed lotto barista meddle lancet bureau forgone treadmill clef-to-precision

connive traduce while stampede reluctance goad motto least immediacy pre-clude mode study matinee sleuth improbable lucidity not ask suffice gap-

ing selector wits over montage breakage lineage—tools of contrast sufficing ludic pram overside meow random clubhouse definitive language meaning torus villa

nelle to combine watershed inroad butane fluidity emaciate addle paramita eagerly scientific avenue asleep other-waves notion from wider glassware dub sniffle trapeze litigant merrily etch pleonastic volunteerism trinket lorgnette waiting succor bluster omit sigh north-ern answer blunt calcify contrastive im-

manence tutoyer simulacra debonair mode convene return salutation mode scruple ahoy bundling meddle baggage tropism blunder improve satori butane

crux slake fortitude imperial coronet lan-guages mildness aware of protectorate blind hamper vineyard slickly presentation emerge allow current lasso tonic

reluctant meringue thanking you eti-quette larynx battalion marionette smog-filled island modicum prone curious to entrance where precisely igno-

rance transits möebius leaning ceiling wharf detailed lightly tatter the curiously proclaim gestural immensity opaque lin-eate snifter lineate happiness letterboxes agreeable mutate oddity slamdunk rosary behavior as much finial snare drifter quasi preclude collectivity immersing capitulate

grade mutely surfacing errata middling pre-
clude mode sufficing paral-

lels démodé treasures retreading surfaces
those providing suddenly sutra-litigant
mile-high merrily fealty certification least
threading amnesia bluster imagine clash

nurtures simplicity engulf returnable
themes earlobe gaffer niobium waitings
from either forecast duet circumstantial re-
curring accuracy blowhard dynasty

ichor sluff clasticity blanket sine qua non
laughter utterly root sagacious genitive
assail proclivity supper tandem silencing
witnesses delft mannerisms nth currently

precise that negotiates elides meanders fa-
cilitates nearby through preponderance
einsam tread burins weavers those there
burgeoning supporting andiron cabinet

warrior blank ghost rattan pirouette also
mannerist ale scud presume eerie cackle
anapest neuron traduce litigant eloge
threaded mode prochain defamation

lesser blink snug refurbishing relaxations emergent capitulate meddling pampers lariat snuffle negotiate fontanelle neural cubbyhole fascinate orbit graded medley

oleander surfaces ballast negotiate balance recursive amplitude suction renga sudden asemic opal migraine rooftop fanzine addle aficionado geist orphic

sanguine skank verbatim evolutionary blister commedia theologic engine leisure pristine calligraphy font asleep neoprene acacia demure petallism negotiate

midas eocturne academe vigilance per-petuate situate medallist arachnid least northerly penuche daring bookish varie-tal surmise poked vaccine traction elite

affetuoso repatriate sedimentary clubhouse putter nascent hub nutmeg allot bivalve emo transept collapse redux perpetua nightly sobriquet misericorde willingly focus cape snifter wall tones fleshed grandly proclaim edict release versional combinatorial geiger slit elite lite medallist gustatory bison gelid ransack im-

merse gosling rancidity proclaim defunct fallow perchance damask gifted malady ousia tardis preclude occiput matte slight bean-town easily arranges willowly vint-

ner appelation grip grateful wider onslaught eprouve night-fallen sacerdotal loutish enigma tortilla escrow plaint varietal mendicant bobtail entrail genies

fenugreek sudden otherwise apparition leisure chthonic principal neuron sly endure lastly prize ampoule guardedly surmise agape grandee sullen dilettante

somnambulist velour acid gifted sonata redux pave sleight fender siphon easel cortege massive alick gentile anaconda geek iteration elision tones oblique tenac ity node alpaca rename sniffle aphasic velour immediacy prelude another anode materialist graphic enlist demode precise valedictory illogic snail versal empty grin

solace smelter assert valedictorian feudal loquacity immerse vital quota peach-tree spurious lumbar oxide adobe connive recur complicate sample networks ges-

tural pittance laborite implode circuitry valedictorian fontanelle bounce daring moodswing relocate dint orbital selection labor neigh saliva deterrent nascar

buttress gecko damper slur grandee ingot muffin tiger ultrafine escape rulers quandry motley chorus definitive beggar drape l'eau escadrille potion scrape foot

deux con machina ingredient acclaim nightfallen capricious effulgence rote sacrifice tartan iffy neon either walled gentle saith winsome iterate tension is land silence ontology provinder shifts venite asleep guttutral quota modus per rapport ascension torus role pleaser cord awhile finesse realitized empty onward

settle oneself neither aegean propriety acme cooper sanitize lasso goaded mirror cane sabra snippet remotely curator earlier warmer also parse gelid machinery

glottal imaging remake normal quarry snapper island genies fiduciary nebbishes inchoate scurry nestle behav-iorist graffiti narrative lucent bludgeon girth assur-

ance glitz presumptuous goat school show igloo proclivity modest rise myrhh thymus ghastly proclivity thrice borax culvert replay neamoins elite gratitude

lesser agronomy sylph pandemonium echo traduce open-side gnash iguana clutter steers apeing amount fantasy took glimmerati lope nearly borough streaming ask gingerly aporia unclear sturdy immense presume clobber nausea spiritual negotiate motto scampi rereward reward gurgitate compulse elate porce-

lain stoic amounting telco vanish calisto barista gavel regale imperial negator silence accidie amount least ossificate mallow binary aural quattro word ironic

genus felicitous emotional settee leaning actual erasure gavel repeat nascar bulletin harvest mitten sleek burrow mote garb leisure graffiti poseur panache em-

bezzle imperiacy panache dodgem bulletin might nook tenacious alarm grapple diffierent gulf homeroom alias butters genus befuddle which waver directive

verbatim iris inward pylon  limbic reload goner allot returnibles deign legate motion slippery grit denier bluster omit vanish tentative preclude elbow dossier gamete bavarder milling ghat buttress show-down politizc muse nth vogue symbiant evolute sombre dasein gloriously predicate masked involute grammaturge

brulant viscera tonnage lotus neither ballast voiceover collapsed deterrents vehicle nothing presence tool denizen precocious integer qaali oggi snuggle

hushed presently motionlessly occasion telling spansule demoiselle granite atlantis veracity plug wherewith aware boing risotto majorette crachet visor plateau

simplicity eachnessless mode scrumptious lean-to surfaces lecture oval peristalsis breakfast ibby craint virgule collarbone garcon vigilance bitternut

agitprop remove allotment bivalve non-contradictory ultramarine favoritism gabardine etch slow-sided boggle mainsail voicemail permafrost gamete bulletin latinate improbably outré gash immensely turgid venial eeriest overhead opaque mullion hogwash tutoyer mica break engine retina slicers trampoline

grind sucrose vastly improbable ousia fantasy reaching contour gap sulk binaural widen utmost genus transient vale occiput rallentando array frequency en-

tirety finial oneself prevaricate wide manners engulf guardian repatriate cease gulf pax greetings abrogate mirror fotomat neither bouree nsaid galactic

eagle lateral nugget relax opaque lenders finesse vineyard innerspring actual temerity aspect bright mocha otherwave milling quotient slack genitive rerun

sleuth immode contrarian peas while voiced reflector than there as kinship relegate orbital mosquito vanish prochain debut oust roller brogue samplers gnostic valence threadless barge dossier vocalize permafrost ludic venezia dollop frank senescent metallic gramophone cluster verbatim impersonal combines traduce

valuable wires deluge rawhide gallon hatcheck lipsync feisty borrower lawdy perimeter calliope sensor transience gaping relapse outré vache gaffer plural

mindset teeteering behest about-face edifice define scramble rebut etape shed not realitizers genies trimming alit cavernous oreilles brunt facetious mortise

gab sluice framing expertise nee engage also-realitizers egg-nog wham slowly nothingly motif between caveat sinistrate volunteers felicitous replacement remov

ers camel boggle rename vinyl periscopeastive least energetic sulking poseur environment accuracy potter sa-gacious certitude iffy changes infancy

prosaic acknowledge build nsaids bevel
hampering scans deterrent capitulating
melisma tureen caveat dint offhand seem-
ly precise midstream culpable vetement

systematic fill oversight eigentum hoopla
concretism imprecision corrigible trestle
buttress capillary extrema vignette aporia
eggshell mode aloe vessel caterwaul pit-

tance scuttle models wooden shofar but-
tons empty psycholog desktop rally coni-
fer waitsafff halibut scrutinizes neoprene
dauggerrotypic saveur neoprana verba-

tim scansiou deploy nebbish mode scuffle
trapeze etology jumping erasire blockage
muddling addenda roleplayeracoustic
vees midding epoche reach other signage

replica genie aleut finessed illbience
madeline capitulate inverse present vigil
sipping zot elbow mindstylism copious
treadmill loquacious threefold maven

harrows ill-intentional bursar evidential commerce silence ictus relata modes in-query motorcade bromeliad uegotiator iepidenic heard grammar button sedi-

mentary variable quasi kaleidoscope var-iably oceanside rendering zoo-phobic delay matinee scree grafter immediacy publican vigilant fontanelle nightfall

ipso facto delay communicative language dwelling warranty soap conduit jimmy-ing alarmed goer shelf noggin sandeesh callow treadmill surfaces deluge

reminder saltpeter wanes euphonic vas-cularity derives motorcade zapping crip-ple misericorde island infancy defunct imaginary precisely nothing lissome

remode démodé additive motored widely throughput thank scenario crown ratchet umbrella quarantine elongations beefs entity noster middling cyanotype ingenious reflection deploy gravelox temperpester arrive contuse ionic least nebbish tension wanderlust specification at least historic gestalt avarice bearing no mode

sterno nova appaloosa waiting showdown rinse prolate modicum ignorant half-alert saith buddle campers metricity advantageous combine relocate middle

leverage hottest neither window lasso prudent caliper rawhide listener zero ontic zone fruitful imagination melody voiceover appeasement iota least scenar-

io pebbles container request other nascent diameter buoy chemin variant appeasement milligram neither aprille tenacity ousia threefold languages tureen

alabaster additive mea culpa reload immerse trepidation merely otherwide precisely various contexts steering caribou relocation evidence op cit sammulgen reign separative quota mode springfold byline ghostly prana mosquito navel warming prasada mollify scenario vale arrondisement brogue lotus abrogate in-

visible wanderers delight entitlement negativity prescient demiurge land-ho vehicle fantast array broken sounds like heist gravity scolded offhand lineate

bungalow demand urgency volunteer nominal tirade sassing listen augury palladium scree variable ousia controlee avail media noche threefold snifter wan-

derer lisp ave martinet haves shortfall attitude leas neuron scumble reticule edifice imperious latinate suggests pedestal metal varsity opaque millefois tra

duces nit sitcom parish nths edifice rawhide mindstyle naivete lurks rally douce preclude suprema intellectual minus del uge brilliance emit presentational genitive rogue lossless tarry ousia mainsail crux foible treehouse itemizers galantine demure vanishing scenario irreal parlance music alarum gegnheit settle wan-

desking fantasia burro customary opaque obsidian needle coldness imperial winderer railing negotiators begotten siddhis meow genial presence necessary

illbient camper snail foresting varsity insectivorous matinee waiting preventable otherwise denial feisty watershed ontic lancet widget relocate eitherly nat-ural

conifer situant brook vestigial sine quaff midrange nonet lotus evaporate delay ousia bevy hexagon stunt languid esplanade tisque trans-farm oppression dull

windless foible titulary nominal voicemail precisely while expansion urges nibble reaching sundry vacancies oblique tenacity node alpaca rename sniffle aphasic velour immediacy prelude another anode materialist graphic enlist demode precise valedictory illogic snail versal empty grin solace smelter assert valedictorian feudal

loquacity immerse vital quota peachtree spurious lumbar oxide adobe connive recur complicate sample networks ges-tural pittance laborite implode circuitry

valedictorian fontanelle bounce daring moodswing relocate dint orbital selec-tion labor neigh saliva deterrent nascar buttress gecko damper slur grandee in-

got muffin tiger ultrafine escape rulers quandry motley chorus definitive beggar drapeau edcadrille potion scapefoat deux con machina ingredient acclaim night-

fallen capricious effulgence rote sacrifice tartan iffy neon either walled gentle saith winsome iterate tension island silence ontology provinder shifts venite asleep guttutral quota modus perpetual zap feisty inroad crokery heeding languages imminence allies rapport ascension torus role pleaser cord awhile finesse realitized

umpty onward settle oneself neither aegean propriety acme cooper sanitize lasso goaded mirror cane sabra snippet remotely curator earlier warmer also parse

gelid machinery glottal imaging remake normal quarry snapper island genies fiduciary nebbishes inchoate scurry nestle behaviorist graffiti narrative lucent

bludgeon girth assurance glitz presumptuous goat sehool show igloo proclivity modest rise myrhh thymus ghastly proclivity thrice borax culvert replay neamoins elite gratitude lesser agronomy slyph pandemonium echo traduce openside gnash iguana clutter steering amount fantasy took glimmerati lope nearly borough steaming ask gingerly aporia unclear sturdy immense presume clobber nausea spiritual negotiate motto scampi regurgitate compulse elate porcelain stoic amount

ing telco vanish calisto barista gavel regale imperial negator silence accidie amount least ossificate mallow binary aural quattro sword ironic genus felici

tous emotional settee leaning actual erasure gavel repeat nascar bulletin harvest mitten sleek burrow mote garb leisure graffiti poseur panache embezzle

imperiacy panache dodgem bulletin might nook tenacious alarm grapple diffierent gulf homeroom alias butters genus befuddle which wave directive

verbatim iris inward pylon limbic reload goner allot returnables deign legat motriu slippery grit denier bluster omit vanish tentative preclude elbow dossier gamete bavarder milling ghat buttress showdown politic muse nth vogue symbiant evolute sombre dasein gloriously predicate masked involute grammaturge

brulant viscera tonnage lotus neither ballast voiceover collapsed deterrents vehi- cle nothing presence tool denizen precocious integer qaali oggi snuggle

hushed presently motionlessly occasion telling spansule demoiselle granite atlantis veracity plug wherewith aware boing risotto majorette crachet visor plateau

simplicity eachnessless mode scrumptious lean-to surfaces lecture oval peristalsis breakfast ibby craint virgule collarbone garcon vigilance bitternut

agitprop remove allotment bivalve noncontradictory ultramarine favoritism gabardine etch slow-sided boggle mainsail voicemail permafrost gamete bulletin latinate improbably outre gash immensely turgid venial eeriest overhead opaque mullion hogwash tutoyer mica break engine retina slicers trampoline grind

sucrose vastly improbable ousia fantasy reaching contour gap sulk binaural widen utmost genus transient vale occiput rallentando array frequency entirety finial

oneself prevaricate wide manners engulf gordian repatriate cease gulf pax greetings abrogate mirror fotomat neither bouree nsaid galactic eagle lateral nugget

relax opaque lenders finesse vineyard innerspring byline cob steering behest about-face edifice define scramble rebut etape shed not realitizers genies trimming alit cavernous oreilles brunt facetious mortise gab sluice framing expertise nee engage also-realitizers eggnog wham slowly nothingly motif between caveat sinistrate volunteers felicitous replacement removers camel boggle rename vinyl periscope contrastive least energetic sulking poseur environment accuracy potter sagacious certitude

iffy changes infancy prosaic acknowledge build nsaids bevel hampering scans deterrent capitulating melisma tureen caveat dint offhand seemly precise midstream

culpable vetement systematic fill oversight eigentum hoopla concretism imprecision corrigible trestle buttress capillary extrema vignette aporia eggshell

mode aloe vessel caterwaul pittance scuttle models wooden shofar buttons empty psychology desktop rally conifer waitsafff halibut scrutinizes neoprene dauggero-

typic saveur neoprana verbatim scansiou deploy nebbish mode scuffle trapeze etology jumping erasire blockage muddling addenda roleplayeracoustic vees midding epoche reach other signage replica genie aleut finessed illbience madeline capitulate inverse present vigil sipping zot elbow mindstylism copious

treadmill loquacious threefold maven harrows ill-intentional bursar evidential commerce silence ictus relata modes inquery motorcade bromeliad negotiator

iepidenic heard grammar button sedimentary variable quasi kaleidoscope variably oceanside rendering zoo-phobic delay matinee scree grafter immediacy

publican vigilant fontanelle nightfall ipso facto delay communicative language dwelling warranty soap conduit jimmying alarmed goer shelf noggin sandeesh callow treadmill surfaces deluge remind

er saltpeter wanes euphonic vascularity derives motorcade zapping cripple misericorde island infancy defunct imaginary precisely nothing lissome remode demodé additive motored widely throughpur thank scenario crown ratchet umbrella quarantine elongations beefs entity noster middling cyanotype ingenious reflec-

tion deploy gravelox temper-pester arrive contuse ionic least nebbish tension wanderlust specification at least historic gestalt avarice bearing no mode sterno

nova appaloosa waiting showdown rinse prolate modicum ignorant alfert saith buddle campers metricity advantageous combine relocate middle leverage hottest

neither window lasso prudent caliper rawhide listener zero ontic zone fruitful imagination melody voiceover appeasement iota least scenario pebbles container request other nascent diameter buoy chemin variant appeasement milligram neither aprille tenacity ousia threefold languages tureen alabaster additive mea culpa reload immerse trepidation merely otherwide precisely various contexts steering caribou relocation evidence op cit sammulgen reign separative quota mode springfold byline ghostly prana

mosquito navel warming prasada mollify scenario vale arrondisement brogue lotus abrogate invisible wanderers delight entitlement negativity prescient demiurge

land-ho vehicle fantast array broken sounds like heist gravity scolded offhand lineate bungalow demand urgency volunteer nominal tirade sassing listen

augury palladium scree variable ousia controlee avail media noche threefold snifter wanderer lisp ave martinet haves shortfall attitude leas neuron scumble

reticule edifice imperious latinate suggests pedestal metal varsity opaque millefois traduces nit sitcom parish nths edifice rawhide mindstyle naivete lurks

rally douce preclude suprema intellectual
minus deluge brilliance emit presenta-
tional genitive rogue lossless tarry ousia
mainsail crux foible treehouse itemizers

galantine demure vanishing scenario ir-
real parlance music alarum gegnheit set-
tle wan desking fantasia burro customary
opaque obsidian needle coldness imperi-

al wanderer railing negotiators begotten
siddhis meow genial presence necessary
illbient camper snail foresting varsity in-
sectivorous matinee waiting preventa-ble

otherwise denial feisty watershed ontic
lancet widget relocate eitherly natural
conifer situant brook vestigial sine quaff
midrange nonet lotus evaporate delay

ousia bevy hexagon stunt languid espla-
nade tisque trans-farm oppression dull
windless foible titulary nominal voicemail
precisely while expansion urges nibble

reaching sundry vacancies gremlin portend genitive orator seethe calzone pebble grateful rouletted unclear burro banish nebbish quanta omicron variable

wanderlist avant neither wampum loquacious totalitarian middle remote absinthe moebius cactus lotto decentrism parlance media noche garage motion

least voluble coriander breath inner breathe mod scrutinize absolutism foghorn motivate lean-to suggesting rule aside mammal connote gainsaid brillian

tine avant element saison duress mail route academic lucent blood notion leaning correct regale ligament barter sobriety barn-sale gullible removal pirouette image motionless agreeable image reptile sack preclude vanish deterrent calypso imitate look serpentine caviar abolish material unwieldy dossier mainsail behemoth neither wrapped unyielding vari ant celebrate sanitize mallow geheben sanctify broke broken small choice amethyst cairn sbicksaal metier vanish pitcher shastra wilt ondine separatism ingest

reopen suddenly porcelain shover byte humulin certes factored mainsail brooked utterance debut tantrum cola tirroir estragon nths blood rotor valence

threaded melody seldom malestrom comment sachet thereins coldly sachet once activate loiter planetary urges grotesque maximal deluge frank shofar assail

fend oleander hatch wry pellet cursory gumshoe cesium blackening shoeshine degree imitate leaning shunt relache until results vulnerably coif demesne throttle

caftan remove alien sorbet maraschino dealers humdrum plutocracy hub offered milling cranium defensive presume tread coverlet mindstylism each vector traduce empty slants geboren standard ghostly perma-lucent grosses transience blood-red motorcraft emptor smashing coefficients eluctably mortise-coined small

talkers elder-wise prosaic tarantella non-politic adventure sample graffiti least mainstay pursuit echo traipse scabbard vehicle loiter ballast otherwise gauche

eglise common-sided awful pursuit emptor neo-transience itemizes borax loiter impulse nascence debut languaged maroon evaluate loiter fly-way governance

estragon neat conifer rallentando parcel urreal cede mindlessly threaded masquerade voiceover plural tardis veneer slack renew peppered vassal infirmity

calibrate soot networking language side-real bulk evidence leaning realization borealis eggless utter-loiter marrow shriek cactus either wandered blast tone scrutinize labors bleach vouchsafe frankly plait renovate architect multiple gab slight naive which dis-isolate communicant-prone maison d'etre avant migrant

palisade imperious gavel selenium candor bog fontanelle leniency produit gusto thunder liaison alacritous melodic sufferance bibliot quorum torpor edifice lancet

tappet relocate elsewhere downstairs lotto hammer place-board scenario muttering cairn standpoint vessel plastic momentums walrus coincide lariat plane-

tary lectern salsa bittern commotion sleuth alertly grace poitrine carom batter lightly plaudit emotional scabbard infiltrate byline cob steering behest about-

face edifice define scramble rebut etape shed not realitizers genies trimming alit cavernous oreilles brunt facetious mortise gab sluice framing expertise nee engage also-realitizers eggnog wham slowly nothingly motif between caveat sinistrate volunteers felicitous replacement removers camel boggle rename vinyl per-

iscope contrastive least energetic sulking poseur environment accuracy potter sagacious certitude iffy changes infancy prosaic acknowledge build nsaids bevel

hampering scans deterrent capitulating melisma tureen caveat dint offhand seemly precise midstream culpable vetement systematic fill oversight eigentum hoopla

concretism imprecision corrigible trestle buttress capillary extrema vignette aporia eggshell mode aloe vessel caterwaul pittance scuttle models wooden shofar but

tons empty psychology desktop rally conifer waitsaff halibut scrutinizes neoprene dauggerotypic saveur neoprana verbatim scansion deploy nebbish mode scuffle trapeze etology jumping erasire blockage muddling addenda roleplayer acoustic vees midding epoche reach other signage replica genie aleut finessed

illbience madeline capitulate inverse present vigil sipping zot elbow mindstylism copious treadmill loquacious threefold maven harrows ill-intentional bursar

evidential commerce silence ictus reltata modes inquery motorcade bromeliad uegotiator iepidenic heard grammar button sedimentary variable quasi kaleido-

scope variably oceanside rendering zoophobic delay matinee scree grafter immediacy publican vigilant fontanelle nightfall ipso facto delay communicative

language dwelling warranty soap— conduit jimmying alarmed goer shelf noggin sandeesh callow treadmill surfaces deluge reminder saltpeter wanes euphonic vascularity derives motorcade zapping cripple misericorde island infan cy defunct imaginary precisely nothing lissome remode démodé additive

motored widely throughput thank scenario crown ratchet umbrella quarantine elongations beefs entity noster middling cyanotype ingenious reflection deploy

gravelox temper-pestic arrive contuse ionic least nebbish tension wanderlust specification at least historic gestalt avarice bearing no mode sterno nova appa

loosa waiting showdown rinse prolate modicum ignorant alfert saith buddle campers metricity advantgeous combine relocate middle leverage hottest neither

window lasso prudent caliper rawhide listener zero ontic zone fruitful imagination melody voiceover appeasement iota least scenario pebbles container request other nascent diameter buoy chemin variant appeasement milligram neither aprille tenacity ousia threefold languages tureen alabaster additive mea

culpa reload immerse trepidation merely otherwide precisely various contexts steering caribou relocation evidence op cit sammulgen reign separative quota

modes springfold byline ghostly prana mosque to navel warming prasada mollify scenario vale arrondisement brogue lotus abrogate invisible wanderers de-

light entitlement negativity prescient demiurge land-ho vehicle fantast array broken sounds like heist gravity scolded offhand lineate bungalow demand ur-

gency volunteer nominal tirade sassing listen augury palladium scree variable ousia controlee avail media noche threefold snifter wanderer lisp ave martinet haves shortfall attitude leas neuron scumble reticule edifice imperious latinate suggests pedestal metal varsity opaque millefois traduces nitre sitcom parish nths edific rawhide mindstyle naivete lurks rally douce preclude suprema

intellectual minus deluge brilliance emit presentational genitive rogue lossless tarry ousia mainsail crux foible treehouse itemizers galantine demure vanishing

scenario irreal parlance music alarum gegnheit settle wan desking fantasia burro customary opaque obsidian needle coldness imperia wanderer railing nego-

tiators begotten siddhis meow genial presence necessary illbient camper snail foresting varsity insectivorous matinee waiting preventable otherwise denial

feisty watershed ontic lancet widget relocate eitherly natural conifer situant brook vestigial sine quaff midrange nonet lotus evaporate delay ousia bevy hexagon stunt languid esplanade tisque trans-farm oppression dull windless foible titulary nominal voicemail precisely while expan sion urges nibble reaching sundry vacan-

cies gremlin portend genitive orator seethe calzone pebble grateful rouletted unclear burro banish nebbish quanta omicron variable wanderlast avant nei-

ther wampum loquacious totalitarian middle remote absinthe moebius cactus lotto decentrism parlance media noche garage motion least voluble coriander

breath inner breathe mod scrutinize absolutism foghorn motivate lean-to suggesting rule aside mammal connote gainsaid brilliantine avant element saison

duress mail route academic lucent blood notion leaning correct regale ligament barter sobriety barn-sale gullible removal pirouette image motionless agreeable image reptile sack preclude vanish deterrent calypso imitate look serpentine caviar abolish material unwieldy dossier mainsail behemoth neither wrapped un-

yielding variant celebrate sanitize mallow geheben sanctify broke broken small choice amethyst cairn sbicksaal metier vanish pitcher shastra wilt ondine sepa-

ratism ingest reopen suddenly porcelain shover byte humulin certes factored mainsail brooked utterance debut tantrum cola tirroir estragon nths blood

rotor valence threaded melody seldom malestrom comme sache thereins coldly sachet once activate loiter planetary urges grotty maximus deluge frank shofar

assail fend oleander hatch wry pelllet cursory gumshoe cesium blackening shoeshine degree imitate leaning shunt relache until results vulnerably coif de mesne throttle caftan remove alien sorbet maraschino dealers humdrum plutocrach hub offered milling cranium defensive presume tread coverlet mindstylist each

vector traduce empty slants geboren standard ghostly permalucent grosses transience blood-red motorcraft emptor smashing coefficients eluctably mortise-

coined small talkers elderwise prosaic tarantelle non-politic adventure sample graffiti least mainstay pursuit echo traipse scabbard vehicle loiter ballast

otherwise gache eglise common-sided awful pursuit emptor neotransience itemizes borax loiter impulse nascence debut languaged maroon evaluate loiter flyway

governance estragon neat conifer rallentando parcel urreal cede mindlessly threaded masquerade voiceover plural tardis veneer slack renew peppered vassal infirmity calibrate soot networking language sidereal bulk evidence leaning realization borealis eggless utter-loiter marrow shriek cactus either wandered

blast tone scrutinize labors bleach vouchsafe frankly plait renovate architect multiple gab slight naive which dis-isolate communicant-prone maison d'etre avant

emigre palisade imperious gavel seleni um candor bog fontanelle leniency produit gusto thunder liasion alacritous melodic sufferance bibliot quorum tor-

por rdifice lancet tappet relocate elsewhere downstairs lotto hammer placeboard scenario muttering cairn standpoint vessel plastic momentums walrus

coincide lariat planetary lecturn salsa bittern commotion sleuth alertly grace poitrine carom tatter lightly plaudir emotionale scabbard infiltrate eidos lapidary glean porcelain dna column nascent durable infinity largesse plotted random selenium gaffer ply sift hemp shellac buttress caveat sine qua nodular foible ren-

dezvous lorry ascii double venusian cairn placard traduce fois threefold majoram collar bone sedimentation eloge midrange afterthought ictus malleably cor-

sage finial combinational modes scruple until remodel hops candle inclination versification leonine activist mollusk brocade impressario gradience employ

yammer clout impressario dasein galleon vascular ply entourage comprehension tablet garish dramaturge lasso nefarious laguna dreadlocks agape smart vehicle

commotion bravo litter feisty horlogerie banish cuffed lorgnette simple ampersand versification ampoule detergent aegis hoard slate dimly capuchin veep agonize staple redo also renege douce batter aloha challenger refuel cuff mandala proclaim tenuto averaging molar book apse trout levitate pulsar bureau

vidalya modes sgraffito nosegay blue redact vinyl agapanthus viable lean-to erasure addenda curve spatial moorish elemental pleasantry energetic involution

pinafore tangible allegro cosine practical maven plyed space palaver boson grapple ingredient versify betweening leis doritos calypso tangiblyousia threefold torte im-

balance byline major inverse untidy sanctify eloquence deterrent garish blunt reasonable finesses gemaceous dolor verbatim capable outtake mindlessness

avail provender context geboren lassi neoprene indexical migrate pimento ghastly disapportionment global fair-weather adjacent bavardez plotting specious leaning trend-to network gingerly application listless vein assail paramour hasp venite amount brain garage mitten acclaim proceed far-reaching logarithm

merci thirst dans oedipus basinet vaisseau reveal chisel nutshell headless remote cairn ballast neither waldorf mindful lament mirage pouce debit once

nein calvary seekers liaison plastic bargain crone deutsch agreeable lipsync felicitous emptor averaging leniency nths wearings swelter vandal finder asleep

yodel avid relocate nosegay czarina bucolic gamete oreilles demure alit vilanelle precisely grammatically noes gingivitis least umpire altimate vanish preclude answer iamb culpable roleplayer nths bold auvergne pylon nib strut alit hem smart fallen bitumen lair stadium tartar milling foible grateful seige earliest our shorn neon parade silliness avid marmor ecru ghastly preclosure once barter mindful era mundane etch camber gymnasium aye surety beyond rinforzando pliable camber geist react novus cactus

waitings gleeful marching elastic photon snippet cloud haphazard meltaway pirouette stump kirtan sublime flourish typical moustache voible rooftop asleep

voiced inner satisfy matinee altimate bingo random serum babble eon scholar vinyl sporadic neither vanish island miscue oleander viable corrective image

seethe maison calcify tease officious relax vent sift zone fontanelle witless naïve borrower nova merciful relocate nibble traduce which veneer porcelain commotion lot eloge aside manifold jut mimic valise proem collaborate orbit lastly noggin vacancy predilection framing sleuth answerings weal imbibe cluster foible raptor inversion caesura dulcet meaningful remake bluster sniffle nimble hiphop bolero brunt sliders quack noon ghost disant bean goaded intext calls dna epicure dns eigentum dial foresting plain

engulf tangibility gape duplex modify garnish vehicle doubts redacting vecu those pebbled brocades métier nascent volition aleut margarine aslant opaque

paradox weaving mire asleep tomorrow's wakefulness pomegranate valence pirouette snow-falling deprecate memento mori treatment soap conscience toot

whinny niter aslan itemizers focus threefold feign blurring etiquette marjoram bulletin ousia territorial cog material name mainspring release coronet vigi

lance brooked enable dulcet brut sample redo incentive lastings elite sailboat merge variable wide convenient altimate cnough simplicity eoconut accroche note vaiable meander snicker wampum oust graffiti spoke madhut piazzola dredge asleep widen ruddeely poseur vermicelli umpteenth vanitas bureaucracy oeuf glad

rag mulled nestle viaduct mollify kept uptowns finder effigy finessed prochain vidalya proclivity embouchure deus ex machina volunteerism snide preoccupy

valence earthly morningside vanguard-ism precisely commonsense parochi-al debutante amiss degree arrow bucolic demonstrate villanelle

normalization borrower vente cacophony genitive swaps vein chrysalis debouche in-gest voila than processual remodification oulipo vane offering wind discourse

than that folderol amity prevent nova ironic von tappet wcdded moitie aleut omnivesal proof-trot miscible tread sei-zure bavardez neither eidos effete lotto spaciously demiurgency politic vat slim miscible demote reload pierce sandstorm vile pratfall eigentum threadless ipseity persuasive attaché nomos calypso ham

mering such therein calling nominal presence violin centrism absolutist emotional coven tenebres seldom remote accuracy wherewhy ozone presumption

lossless shark volition ebb situate non entitlement cavort boardroom capture up imperious globe nitrate ennui nacht emeritus sonic palaver midrange toot

veneer polka kudo yammer tested mosque vital modify geometry bookish viaduct breakwater silliness blarney zone captain defined lacuna delightful haptic

over school saith mirror captivate lotus energetic laconic deutsch sprig happiness wanderer ghostly claque zillionaire crustacean hookish veer anchorite cairn busquer mammoth vignette willowy image reliquary bottleneck hadron silk verbatim andiron mantra selector baud filament thickly basalt middling vanishes

deterrent acsii boardroom gamey bagged traduce milling vanguardism pleonasticism widely sake remodel another vingt equalize emptor eeriest valence commis-

sariat vamp snifter harmonic coldness anvil nestling itemizers delta migrate lutenist preclude lists operating conestoga midrange mosquito venture salida

mignon surfactant limitation elasticity oboe answer hardiness labeled misquota different masquerade mullion galleon cut rate somnolence threaded aliment gro

tesquery nascent mosquito dns regulators map swarm gnit harrow slightly normal energetic laissez proclivity than seize toll noster mondial cuckoo dial dromedary atchitect vigilance bottle answer nominally quatrain delay borrower conduce perimeter returnee alto finders within space hidden boat seethe remote

amid ascot remote lagoon nominality zone refuel nasccnt brokered answer vanishing showdown recur suffice tardy nominal snail sedimentataions manifold effigy opaque lotto either wanderer

random geist mannerist gavel homefront referent connote happiness alsos tensile prudence noesis tenderfoot remove aside latinate rubric harass get go aside ham-

per humid ing latte vanquish escadrille migrations elite alit random dance lastly opaque middle earth relay original vestment leit motif alias big qwaali votary

ivory gemacious rennet aperitif vogue sass overhead hurdle mainframe negotiator evidence leaning presumption eileen coefficient waitstaff returnee widen singularity treat mindstuff thorough noes snark billion sizing refuel vingt apse vim vigorous flushed snuff elite mosquito rename mighty promise far-reaching gar-

age pundit elastic emmissary oppose ne-on prize trapeze prana iffiness regale the-atre basinet magnon lasted ultra legume replacer snub neither night infinity dura

ble rabid noesis throw whichever hardly thereof immediacy heated muon throes delta slammer infernal singularity busker oasis platoon neither foregone suave

material quixoticism unearth soap be-fuddle noah milligram outre ocelot dam-ask avant cerise federal sip zot history nimbus elate notebook snifter wanderer

earliest miller haptic emulator variant nsaids butter abacus neoprene gamete elites deterrents emptor canister evi-dence foresting ectoplasm bulletin abrogate gypsum raconteur heliotrope gram-matical elderberry japa neither aileron vacuous telegraphical jitney buttonhead gestural midi lenient gradients

euphonic veritas buttonheart negator ensemble rationale chorus dealership wanderer imperious gender chime rooftop subaltern guacamole budget image

mirages altitude slow vim heist nounal chloride kudo emit nosegay otiose venite asleet ascot while boated shorn anima snail pattern conestoga fendered lasix

gram nil hocket vocal gentile answer brulant corporeal ultrafine seldom beings neominded engulf buffaloed suede alit nsaid snowfallen bibliot ramification

lossless additives miter house glacial butternut lean clarity hand shoe evidene scansion oomph hadron opiate mg-ten while proclaim dour heterogeny enamel nominal guffaw mil haut pellet moderator candor bucolic pander tisane mugshot ibis relaxation becalm draft watershed genders spiraling either

waistcoast mullah broach oedipus gamelan opaque somatic circuitry skeptic sleep incertitude aitreya comparable tonearm vigilance dealer genuine craft

japa scenario aslant boggle trot maisail boatshoe moviegoer allotropic avenir lavish alveolis picador multiple oases centrist beneath snafu novena astrocastic

mode scruple ancestry ancestry bulletin lagoon negator enamel vehemce alto basking avast headwind sez hoops ez fallow zero bolster milehigh overhaul

demiurge sackbut map seizures loaf vehicle nuance bidding walrus ocelot herto fore understood harrow showcard button mimetic valse desktop gnome serenade sportive feasance topic anemone moviegoer qualify neem gratitude lasso grandiose fondling benign horse crowned hemiduster noes probe nil ru

bric mulling tantrum edifice mote qaali networking facile dub tinge raconteur spatial metonymy circuitry lacunae edit verbatim calliope dance nths goldenrod

navigate elan stellate moisture oppress snurl pieta rawhide garden party shy aprille demurs lariat numble root sanitize elan conduit lamentation elapse geist

wanderer dint opaque expanse variable egging operate masala byline hubris leisure benign showcard enfurl connote encircle nougat milling grapheme

snipped avail nonce deleterious null overhaul smitten overhand aleph nervous warming retainer ceiling einsam peptalk voiceover hassock motions elastic vel-lum spanner crosshairs trope snare laissez oasis borrower ninety engulf sanitize turns scree calligramme finial bursar feint calypso one cache gainsay dusk enfonce

double surefire agreements veranda which while stammer pact session seasonable sortilege mainsail paradox curl nefarious raku slim tones coil

temerity cosi qua infinitude quiddity eternal rime absolutism enigmatic listen catcher oasis bloat filliate acme ghost mortem reopen hammerlock ascii dis-

ponsible remedial vellum entity acclimate variously repetition scrub hobnob sitter ossify narrow echelon venial prochain seconding quorum scholiast bug-bear

circuitry belligerent maintenance reoccur balance gestural vivacity blotted snip shorn nasal gridiron almond sienna rapport luncheon graffiti blogwise embroiled answer noster moviegoer contestant eidos wildflower pious affable island elongate modestly parameter midrange cohere humid ing latte vanquish

escadrille migrations elite alit random dance lastly opaque middle-earth relay original vestment leit motif alias big qaali votary ivory gemacious rennet aperitif

vogue sass overhead hurdle mainframe negotiator evidence leaning presumption tileness coefficient waitstaff returnee widen singularity treat mindstuff thor-

ough noes snark billion sizing refuel vingt apse vim vigorous flushed snuff elite mosquito rename mighty promise far-reaching garage pundit elastic em-

missary oppose neon prize trapeze prana iffiness regale theatre basinet magnon lasted ultra legume replacer snub neither night infinity durable rabid noesis throw whichever hardly thereof immediacy heated muon throes delta slammer infernal singularity busker oasis platoon neither foregone suave material quixoticism

unearth soap befuddle noah milligram outre ocelot damask avant cerise federal sip zot history nimbus elate notebook snifter wanderer earliest miller haptic

emulator variant nsaids butter abacus neoprene gamete elites deterrents emptor canister evidence foresting ectoplasm bulletin abrogate gypsum raconteur heli-

otrope grammatical elderberry japa neither aileron vacuous telegraph ical jitney buttonhead gestural midi lenient gradients euphonic veritas buttonheart nega

tor ensemble rationale chorus dealership wanderer imperious gender chime rooftop subaltern guacamole budget image mirages altitude slow vim heist nounal chloride kudo emit nosegay otiose venite asleet ascot while boated shorn anima snail pattern conestoga fendered lasix gram nil hocket vocal gentile answer

brulant corporeal ultrafine seldom beings neominded engulf buffaloed suede alit nsaid snow-fallen bibliot ramification lossless additives miter house glacial but-

ternut lean clarity hand shoe evidence scansion oomph hadron opiate mg-ten while proclaim dour heterogeny enamel nominal guffaw mil haut pellet modera-

tor candor bucolic pander tisane mug-shot ibis relaxation becalm draft water-shed genders spiraling either waist-coast mullah broach oedipus gamelan opaque

somatic circuitry skeptic sleep incerti-tude aitreya comparable tonearm vigi-lance dealer genuine craft japa scenario aslant boggle trot mainsail boatshoe moviegoer allotropic avenir lavish alveolis picador multiple oases centrist beneath snafu novena astrocastic mode scruple ancestry ancestry bulletin lagoon

negator enamel vehemce alto basking avast headwind sez hoops ez fallow zero bolster milehigh overhaul demiurge sackbut map seizures loaf vehicle nuance

bidding walrus ocelot heretofore understood harrow showcard button mimetic valse desktop gnome serenade sportive feasance topic moviegoer qualify neem

gratitude lasso grandiose fondling benign horse crowned hemiduster noes probe nil rubric mulling tantrum edifice mote qaali networking facile dub tinge

raconteur spatial metonymy circuitry lacunae edit verbatim calliope dance nths goldenrod navigate elan stellate moisture oppress snurl pieta rawhide garden party shy aprille demurs lariat numble root sanitize elan conduit lamentation elapse geist wanderer dint opaque expanse variable egging operate masala byline hubris

leisure benign showcard enfurl conote encircle nougat milling grapheme snipped avail nonce deleterious null overhaul smitten overhand aleph nervous

warming retainer ceiling einsam peptalk voiceover hassock motions elastic vellum spanner crosshairs trope snare laissez oasis borrower ninety engulf sanitize

returns scree calligramme finial bursar feint calypso one cache gainsay dusk enfoncé double surefire agreements veranda which/while stammer pact ses-sion/seasonable sortilege mainsail paradox url nefarious raku slim notes green also isness taal midrash genetic lifter align talon falsify reach tensile partook samulgen particulate noesis train-master valise addle imitator nova gitanes ludic eggshell deploy guarantor vehicle demilitarize gnosis tradition a latinate vecu mudsling remodel acinate metallic es-

sence chorus détente mainstay oggi paramita evolute csarina deploy engineers tone erewhon stubby call zone gremlin adjective lacunae deterrent caliphate

modus caftan meringue lab shifty clarionette answering machines in alternative radian pulchritude opaque negator valise transcend acoustic variable merge as-

sume memes refute caloric doubles endgames lundi mardi mercredi valse landless pool fend reanimate acid-free amigo narrow spatula everlast desserts reverse camouflage opaque orangerie medallist vanguard loiter ensemble middle torrent bloodless outré garnet cackle answering relatedness one tone tine overall grimaces brood-warmer connotes tarry crucible language deleta flux neomancer slat hubris refuse aside gallantry poseur general formal sift harmonic lossless garment iterate ludic laughter slot filament nsaids

yet connect mindful immense testament validate modernity claret vinyl landed allowance delay hoopla nitrate milling psalter abundant emulate grab sentiment

voiceover egoity remonstrations candle nodding latrine alacritous grammacy oases gator sanctify agility promontory tiger etiquette asleep readership genus

satyr genesis treaded mallow tendency listener slash red blotto incindary test-tube slanders emotilar offensive promulgate thinner discourse latinate sublate

mode sturdy smelter year-long mindstylism naïve delta möebius blast gangrene mitten scarab fuse reothering sample addle manifold lamentation nolo contention sleuth volume literal snub hammers graduate multis bloodless nowhere multiples delta mixings relearning slowhand perimeter castigate eche-

lon grandiose mitten studious foghorn bison glitterati listed mended salute rampage introit values agora phantasm lucidity captive wakefulness endless gur-

gle animate resultancy impregnates watershed situation electorate stubby holding contrast verification legume immerse ditto capitulate ocular geometry nsiddhis

elite hoard smite align tartan listener foster hundred miter capitulate itness while sparring owlet nsaids etiquette marionette vacuum moorish gallanine neem cal

liope finder siddhi velocity presentable roulette comparison vehicle treadmilling random sturgeon caves dullard utter pincer grapple umbrella mimic reunite fiber wanderer kept mudra human illbient file transience parochial duenna growth peach ghastly repatriate locust valuable tyrant rollerderby anchor sizing ampoule

traduce folio earliest mimetic lots mode sturdy cellophane trending violincello therefore mob styrene gelid nasal curator escadrille potentate omit voir cabriolet

immo prelude anothered close ottoman literal nova geistlich immune zone traduce labor  grit coaxial nebulae transient valse opaque opposing literal noesis traf-

fic feint mountain slight alignment calcify repute milligraph smiling crockery animate columnal presumption evidencing relaché great mountain litotes caliph

oeuvre asemic hearsay integral pittance slack nub echelon vanish parallel mindstyle impede lorry haphazard letterbox darings nominal trait least environ nib snippet remoulade snail predatorial commune triffid elsewise grateful pattern apparition lot snifter wand finesse grade milquetoast nib sleigh ampoule trash

gnit harrow vingt moebius gallantry nominally procedural thrown intellect mindstyle paradise versional tout osmosis reflex context vegetal prolivity othered

imitate least as yoga vouchsafe smelter anchorite cackle opiate vocalize nub snitch lissome translate mirage leitmotif valuation lummox veil paradise levee lat-

inate mignon slumber padded a lot meanders myopically gladden oleander poseur goner alveoli venusian botox valise paradiddle environs letterset manifold

petal skid trot silences denizen presume elate answer billion forest triton calzone breakage molecule adore saith milhausen bottled miter another waiting lossletter officially proclivity absinthe vacancy prolate mode also hearth sleuth fodder masochistic bivalve oceanic meddlesome nonfat fringe rambunctious tape silencers

aficionado least wordless ontic mainsaid pirouette agate molecule porous claque lamentation prelude noestra dial awareness opaque field thought forfeit amplit

mind zoned voila afloat steam infringe pall genome aside laborite meal-tone cross haptic redundancy presumption jet grammaturgy solenoid parcel manifold

foreign operating begin feist uniformal ditto scarab scientic aside lagoon meaning eriss-cross wade ipseity connote rarefied macimimos chiasmus often bibliot

once sortie vascularity fence alt homeroom nasal bested amulet chorus annoooaoe enough umbilical every tenuto saith multi feint reify parson slice game plan night pristine where adjective eerie holiday boundary cling trot evidencing precisely trattoria voiceover haphazard ultra jettison wholly fractured impala

grist heliotrope advantageous mollfy hold huff alyssum planetery collision hammer subdude alterations sobriquet immolate ciliated eerie sestina parsec fire-

cast multiple analog ethereal bottom-feeder plasticity mellow precise cordillra dormancy profligate motions enigmatic where study crisper nailed mohair grem-

lin dossier oases final retro-fictive latitudes tent mainfold vue gnarl wiltings bear shot anchorite northern a collection partook ivory utterance blogger qualitas

fusillade emigre partsong mellow diameter voices dereliction proscenium sluice feint aggregate moon reactioned engine release iguana theirself genant negotiator

**ADDITIONAL PUBLICATIONS available at**

https://www.lulu.com/lunabisonteprods

**Remove A Concept Volume 13**
Peter Ganick, 2012, Luna Bisonte Prods publication

*Drink down sweltering ingots of Ganick attack. He'll shave your morning; you turn up again in raw words.*
-John Pursch

**orientation**
Peter Ganick, 2012, Luna Bisonte Prods publication

*Poet, Sheila E. Murphy, wrote in a haibun for Peter Ganick (read full version at http://ex-ex-lit.blogspot.com): "The word for weeds that should be jewelry makes the yard a globe. The place to pay admission is the mind, where rock formations dry after an overdose of winter." That empty yard is a landfill for every full & generous poem in orientation. Look here to energize the mind's eye and elasticize the sky.*

**untitled poems for a wednesday evening.**
Peter Ganick, 2011, Luna Bisonte Prods publication

*The mind within and beneath these pieces is infinitely shimmering, even as the poet's signature sotto voce consistently asserts itself.* -Sheila E. Murphy

www.ingramcontent.com/pod-product-compliance
Lightning Source LLC
Chambersburg PA
CBHW060425050426
42449CB00009B/2135
*9781938521164*